WHY NOBODY
WANTS TO GO TO
CHURCH
ANYMORE

ACTION PLAN
WORKBOOK FOR YOUR MINISTRY TEAM

Loveland, CO

THOM & JOANI SCHULTZ

Group resources really work!

This Group resource incorporates our R.E.A.L. approach to ministry. It reinforces a growing friendship with Jesus, encourages long-term learning, and results in life transformation, because it's:

Relational—Learner-to-learner interaction enhances learning and builds Christian friendships.

Experiential—What learners experience through discussion and action sticks with them up to 9 times longer than what they simply hear or read.

Applicable—The aim of Christian education is to equip learners to be both hearers and doers of God's Word.

Learner-based—Learners understand and retain more when the learning process takes into consideration how they learn best.

Why Nobody Wants to Go to Church Anymore: ACTION PLAN
Workbook for Your Ministry Team

Copyright © 2014 Group Publishing, Inc.

Visit our website for more small group and church leadership resources: **group.com**

Unless otherwise indicated, all Scripture quotations are taken from the *Holy Bible*, New Living Translation, copyright © 1996, 2004, 2007. Used by permission of Tyndale House Publishers, Inc., Carol Stream, Illinois 60188. All rights reserved.

ISBN 978-1-4707-1654-7

Printed in the United States of America

10 9 8 7 6 5 4 3 2 1   23 22 21 20 19 18 17 16 15 14

INTRODUCTION

Welcome to the Action Plan Workbook for *Why Nobody Wants to Go to Church Anymore*. If you're reading this, chances are you care a lot about the church. So do we!

When it comes to the body of Christ, the first thing we need to remember is that we're all human. If there's a reason so many churches are struggling and failing today, it's because we mortals tend to be rather, well, messy. We all make mistakes. We assume the wrong things. We say the wrong things. We take steps that send us backward. We fail.

Thankfully, we have a God who never fails. A faithful, loving God who calls us his Bride. And God knew exactly what he was doing when he molded us, collectively, into this remarkable entity called the church. Even though God knows we have a tendency to make mistakes, he also knows we have a great capacity to show his love to others. We are *his* body, after all, and through us God accomplishes amazing things.

This Action Plan Workbook is your team's guide to accomplishing two main objectives: 1) discover how your church may be falling short when it comes to truly loving God and others, and 2) explore how you can transform your church into a place of extraordinary, authentic, irresistible love.

As with all Group resources, you can expect to find a healthy amount of interactive experiences built into this workbook. You'll talk with each other. A lot. You'll dig deep into the book *Why Nobody Wants to Go to Church Anymore* and Scripture. You'll engage in experiences together that will open your eyes to unexpected discoveries. And, most importantly, you'll grow closer to God and each other.

Not only will you be *learning* about the 4 Acts of Love, but you'll also be *doing* the 4 Acts of Love as you progress through this workbook. We're firm believers in learning by doing, so you'll get plenty of opportunities to practice real love with real people in every lesson.

These experiences will stretch you. They might make you a bit uncomfortable. They'll cause you to grapple with some pretty tough questions. But along the way, you'll find answers, surprises, and a tangible hope that will stir your heart to action.

Our team spent a lot of time in prayer as we prepared this workbook, and we trust your team will do the same. We believe God is our sole source of power and hope, and every moment you devote to conversation with God is time well spent. Rest assured our team will be praying for you daily as you consider what kind of church you can be in the years ahead.

Thank you for your willingness to jump in, be bold, and embrace the changes that are coming your church's way. Let's have some fun!

Serving Christ together,

Thom & Joani Schultz

WHY NOBODY WANTS TO GO TO CHURCH ANYMORE
ACTION PLAN: Workbook for Your Ministry Team

CONTENTS

How to Use This Workbook 6

Session 1—Looking Inward:
How is our church *really* doing? 9

Session 2—Radical Hospitality:
Are people welcome just as they are? 19

Session 3—Fearless Conversation:
Are thoughts, doubts, and questions welcome? 31

Session 4—Genuine Humility:
Is everyone in our church in this together? 43

Session 5—Divine Anticipation:
Are you ready to connect with God in a fresh way? 55

Session 6—Looking Outward:
What do we do now? 63

Continue the Conversation 75

Resources to Help Your Journey 76

HOW TO USE THIS WORKBOOK

This workbook is designed to be used with a group of people as they discuss action steps in response to the book *Why Nobody Wants To Go To Church Anymore: And How 4 Acts of Love Will Make Your Church Irresistible*. It may be a leadership team, members of a church staff, a Sunday morning Bible class, or a home small group. Anyone who wants to help their church transform into a place of irresistible love will benefit from experiencing the six sessions in this workbook.

Each lesson is organized into the following sections:

Warm Up *(5 minutes)*
This section connects group members with each other through a warm-up, mixer, or opportunity to get better acquainted. It's designed to be fun and informative and sets the tone for the rest of the study.

Follow Up *(5-10 minutes)*
Starting with Session 2 you'll have an opportunity for group members to share any personal discoveries from the previous week's personal challenge.

Open Up *(15-20 minutes)*
In this section group members will dig deeper and begin to make applications from the book *Why Nobody Wants to Go to Church Anymore* to their own life and church.

Look It Up *(15 minutes)*
This section allows group members the opportunity to grapple with the session's key concepts and make personal discoveries.

Wise Up *(10 minutes)*
Here's where group members will work through the biblical application to apply God's Word to the main ideas of each session.

Rise Up *(5 minutes)*

This is the "action step" of the session. Each group member will reflect on how they will live out the session's main message in the week ahead. They'll take on a challenge and share their discoveries the following week.

Wrap Up *(5-10 minutes)*

This section concludes your time together each week with final thoughts from the ideas discussed during the session, as well as a time of prayer.

Training Tips

- Feel free to customize the suggested time schedule. You can allow extra discussion if you'd like to fill a 90-minute class or narrow the focus to shorten to 60 minutes.

- Appoint a facilitator to lead the discussion and follow the training directions.

- Within the six sessions, sections in regular font are meant to be read aloud by the facilitator to the entire group.

- Sections in **bold font** are intended to be read by the whole group.

- Sections within brackets [ ] are directions to the session facilitator and should not be read aloud.

- Be sure each participant has their own workbook to complete the exercises and use as a journal for their discoveries.

- Depending on the size of the group, it's best if group members sit in circles of 4 to 6 chairs or at round tables. The discussion time will be more effective with a smaller group or with pairs when suggested.

- Pray that God will guide and direct the discussion and discoveries of each participant.

- Relax and have fun!

WHY NOBODY WANTS TO GO TO CHURCH ANYMORE
ACTION PLAN: Workbook for Your Ministry Team

Looking Inward:
How is our church *really* doing?

Reminder!

- Sections in regular font are meant to be read aloud by the facilitator to the entire group.

- Sections in **bold font** are intended to be read by the whole group.

- Sections within brackets [ ] are directions to the session facilitator and should not be read aloud.

Warm Up *(5 minutes)*

Thank you for joining us in this journey to discover how we can transform our church into a place of extraordinary, authentic, and irresistible love. We're all in this together!

Let's start this session by getting to know each other a little better. Let's say you were offered a job at six different places: in a police department, on a political action committee, at a theater, at a mortuary, in a seminary, or at a museum. Which one of those would be your first choice? Why would you choose that job?

[Allow everyone in the group to share their answers.]

9

SESSION 1 | Looking Inward:
How is our church *really* doing?

Open Up *(20 minutes)*

Now let's talk about each of these places as they relate to the church. For each building listed in your workbook, we'll read aloud the questions and then have each person discuss their open and honest answers. We'll have about 3 minutes to discuss each type of building.

The Police Station

- Is our church known as a place that stresses the dos and don'ts? Or is it known as a haven for thriving relationships?

The Political Action Committee

- Is our church known as the place where lines are drawn in the sand? Or is it known as the place where people draw together?

The Theater

- Do most people sit and watch a show when they come to our church? Or do they pay attention to each other and grow closer together when they attend?

The Mortuary

- Do people view our church as a solemn place of remembrance? Or do they see it as a vibrant place full of life and growth?

The Seminary

- Does our church spend more of its time and budget on transferring knowledge? Or do we spend more of our budget on growing real relationships with God and others?

The Museum

- Would people describe our church as a place that focuses more on preserving tradition? Or would they describe it as a place that emphasizes growing real-life, everyday relationships?

Look It Up *(15 minutes)*

Let's read this excerpt together from *Why Nobody Wants to Go to Church Anymore:*

> "About 20 years ago, we wrote a book called *Why Nobody Learns Much of Anything at Church: And How to Fix It.* We wanted to be a catalyst to revolutionize Christian education. And to our great surprise, much of the landscape of the way the church teaches the Bible, especially to teens and children, changed. It worked! People of all ages began experiencing the Bible as they never had before. It was a mini revolution!
>
> "But we now realize our laser focus on education was a distraction. That's because faith is not a subject.
>
> "Faith is a relationship…
>
> "Think about that for a moment. Faith is a relationship, not a topic to be studied.
>
> "Once we understood that, our view of what happens at church changed. Completely. And it's opening doors we never even knew existed." (pages 18-19)

Let's talk about that.

- What's your reaction to the statement: "Faith is a relationship, not a topic to be studied"?

- Write down (on a whiteboard or sheet of paper) all the things our church spends its time doing. What percentage of those things are focused on learning? On relationships?

- When the average person comes to our church, how much of their time is spent building relationships? With God? With others?

- Think about the closest relationships in your life. How much of your time with those people do you spend "studying" them versus doing relational things with them? How is that like or unlike our faith relationships?

13

SESSION 1 | Looking Inward:
How is our church *really* doing?

Wise Up *(10 minutes)*

Let's dig into some Scripture together and read Matthew 22:36-40:

> " 'Teacher, which is the most important commandment
> in the law of Moses?'
>
> "Jesus replied, ' "You must love the Lord your God
> with all your heart, all your soul, and all your mind."
> This is the first and greatest commandment. A second
> is equally important: "Love your neighbor as yourself."
> The entire law and all the demands of the prophets
> are based on these two commandments.' "

Now let's talk about these questions:

- People don't go to police stations, theaters, museums, political action committees, mortuaries, or seminaries expecting to be loved. Based on the Scripture we just read, should the church be a place where people can expect to be loved? Why or why not? And what should that love look like?

- Why do you think some churches seem to "lose their way" when it comes to loving people?

- Would most people say they feel genuinely loved after visiting our church? Why or why not? What are two or three things our team could do differently to show God's love to people who come to our church?

- Do you think more people would be inclined to go to church if they knew they would be loved there? Why or why not?

Rise Up *(5 minutes)*

Action Plan Step 1

One of the best ways to discover what people think about our church is, well, to simply ask them!

Here's a challenge for each of us this week:

1. Contact two people: One who regularly attends our church, and one who's been to our church but rarely comes. (Tip: Offer to buy them coffee or dessert, and assure them you just want to catch up and are curious to get their thoughts on a couple of ideas related to our church.)

15

SESSION 1 | Looking Inward:
How is our church *really* doing?

2. During your time together, ask them the following questions. (Tip: Let your friend know that you just want their honest feedback in an effort to make our church a better place. When they share their answers, don't try to tell them why they're wrong or how you might disagree. Accept their feedback graciously.)

- People go to theaters to be entertained, and they go to schools to learn. Why do you think people want to go to church?

- Should people expect to feel loved when they go to church? If so, how do you think that love should be acted out? If not, what should people expect from church?

- Would you say you feel loved after attending a typical service at our church? Why or why not?

- What's something that, if it happened at our church, would make you feel we cared about you?

3. Be sure to thank them for taking the time to meet with you. Let them know that you're excited about the new things God is doing in our church and that their feedback is very valuable in helping us improve our ministry.

Alternative option:

Sometimes it's hard for people to open up and be truly honest with the leaders of their church. If you think this may be the case with your potential interviewees, recruit a small handful of volunteers to conduct the above interviews for you. Have them take notes and report back to the team.

When We Did This

To our amazement everyone who had left our church was thankful somebody cared enough to ask! People want to be noticed and listened to. Note: Resist the urge to get defensive. Listen. That was important to them.

Wrap Up *(5 minutes)*

[Have the group stand together in a circle.]

If you're wearing a wedding ring (or other ring), pull it off your finger (if you can!) and hold it up.

17

SESSION 1 | **Looking Inward:**
How is our church *really* doing?

[Have one of your team members read aloud the following:]

In many ways, our relationship with God is a lot like a marriage. You fall in love, you spend time together and get to know each other, and you do special things for each other. Eventually you make a commitment to that person because you want to spend the rest of your life with him or her. The ring symbolizes that commitment.

We're standing in a circle now. Much like these rings we're holding, this circle symbolizes the way our church has formed a long-lasting bond with each other and God. But it can also be a symbol of how we've turned ourselves inward and not done the most we can to accept those outside our church and show them the full extent of God's love.

Hold your ring in your hand and silently pray for our openness and willingness to discovering the ways, however big or small, that God may want to transform our church.

[Pause for silent prayer.]

Now place your ring back on your finger and join hands as a group. We'll take turns sharing one-sentence prayers aloud for our team's commitment to loving each other.

[Pause for prayers.]

Now let's take turns sharing one-sentence prayers for our team's commitment to loving the people our church wants to reach.

[Pause for prayers.]

Amen!

Next week we're going to explore the first Act of Love: Radical Hospitality. Be prepared to share the results from your interviews during the week. And be ready to explore how Radical Hospitality can make our church irresistible.

Radical Hospitality:
Are people welcome just as they are?

Reminder!

- Sections in regular font are meant to be read aloud by the facilitator to the entire group.

- Sections in **bold font** are intended to be read by the whole group.

- Sections within brackets [ ] are directions to the session facilitator and should not be read aloud.

Warm Up *(5 minutes)*

Welcome back! I appreciate your commitment to helping our church show God's love. This week we're going to be digging into the first of the 4 Acts of Love: Radical Hospitality. Let's start with a simple activity. Please take your driver's license or other form of I.D. from your purse or wallet. Most people don't think their driver's license photo is the best representation of who they are. Let's take turns answering this question:

- What's one thing no one would know about you just by looking at your photograph?

SESSION 2 | Radical Hospitality:
Are people welcome just as they are?

19

Follow Up *(10 minutes)*

Let's take a few minutes to share any interesting discoveries from our personal challenge from last week. We were supposed to interview two people: One who regularly attends our church, and one who has attended but rarely comes. Let's briefly discuss the following questions:

- What's one "ah-ha" you came away with after talking with those two people?

- What insight did those interviews give you about how our church is perceived by people in this community?

When We Did This

We were stunned by the strong emotions expressed. Some were hurt, angry, valued, curious, left out, suspicious. We learned we can't assume we know what people think or feel!

Open Up *(15 minutes)*

"I feel judged" versus "You're welcome just as you are."

All of us have likely experienced times when we didn't feel like we belonged. Maybe there was a time in junior high when you were rejected by certain social groups. Perhaps you attended a dinner party where everyone's cars and clothes were way nicer than yours. Maybe you worked at a job where everyone seemed to clam up whenever you were around.

Let's divide into pairs and take a few minutes to answer this question:

- Tell about a time when you felt like you didn't belong. How did that make you feel about yourself? About the people who didn't accept you?

[After everyone has shared with a partner, take a couple of minutes to have people share a story or two with the whole group.]

All of us have also had times when we felt like we *did* belong. We knew the people around us accepted us for who we were. They didn't care about our weaknesses, our shortcomings, or our faults.

Turn to your partner again and take turns discussing this question:

- Tell about a time when you felt like you were accepted by a group of people. How did that make you feel about yourself? About the people who embraced you?

SESSION 2 | Radical Hospitality:
Are people welcome just as they are?

21

[Again, if some are willing, have people share highlights from a few stories with the rest of the group.]

Considering what we've all experienced with acceptance and rejection, let's discuss the following question:

- Why do you think so many people are judged, condemned, and rejected by people—all imperfect people—in the church?

Look It Up *(15 minutes)*

Let's read this excerpt together from *Why Nobody Wants to Go to Church Anymore:*

> "Jesus says, 'You're welcome just as you are.' Throughout his ministry, Jesus embraced despised prostitutes, cheating tax collectors, smelly fishermen, and all manner of sinners. He reached out and touched the blind, the lame, even the 'untouchables'—the lepers. Jesus opened his arms and welcomed others in such a radical way that the churchy types got pretty ticked! We humans would rather people clean up their act *before* we connect with them. Thankfully, God doesn't think like that." (page 73)

Let's talk about this:

- Chapter 5 of *Why Nobody Wants to Go to Church Anymore* tells the story of when Mike Jones, the male prostitute from the Ted Haggard scandal, came to visit a Lifetree Café session featuring Haggard. What would happen in our church if Mike Jones showed up to a worship service or in one of our Sunday school classes or Bible study groups? Name some specific ways our church would respond to Mike.

- Do you think it's fair that most people (87 percent!) say they feel judged by the church? What do you think Jesus would consider more important: judging people or showing them love? Explain your answers.

- What are some ways people in our community might feel judged by our church?

23

SESSION 2 | Radical Hospitality:
Are people welcome just as they are?

- Describe how our church would be different if everyone were welcome "just as they are."

Wise Up *(10 minutes)*

Let's read aloud this passage from Matthew 7:1-2 together and then discuss the following questions:

> **"Do not judge others, and you will not be judged. For you will be treated as you treat others."**

- What does this Bible passage mean to you?

- How do you think this Scripture applies to how the church should treat all the people within its reach?

- How do you think a Christian justifies judging others in spite of this verse?

Rise Up *(5 minutes)*

Action Plan Step 2

Here's our personal challenge for this week: Take a few minutes sometime in the next few days to write down on a sheet of paper, privately, a list of five reasons someone might not welcome *you* just as you are. Next to that list, write down five things you find yourself judging other people for. Finally, one at a time, cross off each of those 10 things with a red pen. As you cross off each one, write down one way you could counter that rejection with a simple act of love. Take a couple of minutes to connect with God and commit your list to his hands, asking him for the grace to act in love instead of judgment. (Be sure to bring your list with you to next week's session.)

Optional Challenge:

Review the following list taken from chapter 6 of *Why Nobody Wants to Go to Church Anymore* for practical ways to love with Radical Hospitality. Choose **one** of these suggestions as a group and implement one to three things in church **this week.** (If you feel successful, maybe you can try a new one every month.)

- Embrace the power of environment. What can we change in our church to make it a place where people can always expect to grow closer to others?

- Understand the power of language. What "code words" can we eliminate from our church's vocabulary?

SESSION 2 | Radical Hospitality: Are people welcome just as they are?

25

- Take time for befriending. What can we change about our Sunday morning routine to intentionally bring people closer to each other?

- Remember, friends and family bring friends and family. How can we replace generic marketing efforts to invite people to our church with more personal engagement?

- Understand the power of name. What can we do to encourage everyone in our church to learn each other's names?

- Get better acquainted through personal storytelling. How can we incorporate personal sharing into worship services and meeting times?

- The leader sets the tone. What can we as a leadership team do to model Radical Hospitality to each other and the rest of our church?

- Eat together. Food brings people together. How can we move beyond doughnuts and coffee?

- Don't underestimate the power of a smile. (Enough said, right?)

When We Did This

Our leadership team meets every month for Bible study, prayer, and breakfast cooked by our CEO, Thom! When others see leaders respecting and loving each other, it makes a difference.

SESSION 2 | Radical Hospitality:
Are people welcome just as they are?

27

Wrap Up *(5 minutes)*

Take off your shoes and put them in the center of our group. Now pick up one shoe from the pile that won't fit your foot (either too large or too small).

[Have one person in your group read aloud the following:]

Hold the shoe up to your foot. Maybe it's too small. Or too big. Maybe it's a style you would never, ever wear. What would you think if, in order to be accepted by the others in this group, you had to wear this shoe—all the time, with no exceptions? [Pause for 10 seconds.] **How would that make you feel?** [Pause for 10 seconds.] **What would you think of the people who made you wear this shoe?** [Pause for 10 seconds.] **Would you join this group?** [Pause for 10 seconds.]

Now let's put the shoe on the other foot, so to speak. Hold up the shoe again and imagine what it would be like to walk in another person's shoes as they step into our church for the first time. [Pause.] **What would they see as they entered?** [Pause.] **Who would greet them or talk to them?** [Pause.] **How would they fit in if they were different?** [Pause.] **What would be going through their mind as they left?** [Pause for 30 seconds.]

Jesus calls us to love others, not to judge others. Jesus calls us to be his hands—and feet—to those we come in contact with. These shoes represent all the ways we try to make people fit our mold. But if we follow Jesus' example, we'll find ourselves ignoring the shoes and washing those feet, no matter what they look like, where they've been, or even where they might be going.

Now it's time to pray together. Let's have 1 minute of silent prayer, asking God to show us ways to help our church love people and welcome them just as they are.

[Pause for 1 minute of silent prayer.]

Amen!

Next week we're going to explore the second Act of Love: Fearless Conversation. Be prepared to share the results from your weekly challenge with the group. And be ready to explore how Fearless Conversation can make our church irresistible.

SESSION 2 | Radical Hospitality:
Are people welcome just as they are?

29

WHY NOBODY WANTS TO GO TO CHURCH ANYMORE
ACTION PLAN: Workbook for Your Ministry Team

SESSION 3

Fearless Conversation:
Are thoughts, doubts, and questions welcome?

Reminder!

- Sections in regular font are meant to be read aloud by the facilitator to the entire group.
- Sections in **bold font** are intended to be read by the whole group.
- Sections within brackets [ ] are directions to the session facilitator and should not be read aloud.

Warm Up *(5 minutes)*

Welcome! I appreciate your partnership in this Action Plan process. Thanks for giving of your time to serve God and others by being here. Let's start things off this session by taking turns sharing a question. One at a time, we'll each share our responses. We're not going to respond to each person's answer. Just listen to each other.

[If you have a large group, divide into trios to share your answers.]

- If God could give you the answer to one question, what would you ask him? And why are you curious about that?

31

SESSION 3 | Fearless Conversation:
Are thoughts, doubts, and questions welcome?

Follow Up (*5 minutes*)

Let's take a few minutes to share any of our discoveries from our personal challenge from last week. We were challenged to write a list of five ways we're judged and five ways we judge others. Then we were supposed to cross off each of those judgments one by one and write down ways we could replace them with simple acts of love.

Please take out your sheet of paper with your list. Now—rip it up!

- How did it feel to destroy your list of judgments? What have you learned this week about unconditional love?

Open Up (*15 minutes*)

"I don't want to be lectured. You don't care what I think." versus "Your thoughts are welcome; your doubts are welcome."

Chapter 2 of *Why Nobody Wants to Go to Church Anymore* talks about the different ways in which the church has allowed itself to become something other than a place where love and relationships thrive. The seminary format is perhaps the most common example, where churches decide that the dispensation of knowledge is the most important thing they do.

The result? Eighty percent (or more) of a church's time, money, and effort is focused on bringing people into the building to sit quietly and listen to a lecture/sermon. And most likely they will have forgotten virtually everything they heard before they walk out the door. In fact, research says 90 percent will be gone! Poof!

When We Did This

We've asked churchgoers on a Wednesday what they recall from Sunday... you'd be shocked! And they heard good preachers.

But, as research proves, most people don't want to be lectured to. They want to ask questions. They want to share their own thoughts. They want to engage with other people and experience a relationship with God.

They want to love and be loved.

As a group, let's take 2 minutes (someone keep time!) and make a list of topics that our church would never, ever address on a Sunday morning. When we're finished with the list, we'll discuss the following questions.

[Write list of topics on a flip chart.]

- Why do you think churches are afraid to tackle certain subjects? Do you think they're justified?

- Why do you think most churches don't give people an opportunity to ask hard questions?

SESSION 3 | Fearless Conversation:
Are thoughts, doubts, and questions welcome?

- How would our church be different if it were a place of two-way conversations about any given topic, instead of only one-way lectures about biblically "safe" topics where the leader was in control?

- In what ways might people feel more loved if they were given a voice in our church's conversation?

Two-Way Conversation

The simplest way to engage people in a two-way conversation at any time and in any setting—during a sermon, class, or meeting—is simply to ask people to turn to a partner and react to what was just said.

Wise Up *(10 minutes)*

Let's dig into some Scripture together. This is 1 Corinthians 13:7 from *The Message* translation:

> "No matter what I say, what I believe, and what I do, I'm bankrupt without love."

It all comes down to this: Will we choose to love others first and foremost? Or will we continue to insist that filling people with information should be our priority? Let's discuss:

- Some church leaders argue that dispensing biblical knowledge is in itself an act of love. Describe how you think the people in the pews may or may not feel loved by being given a steady stream of informational lectures.

- What do you think it really means to love others? (You may refer to the rest of 1 Corinthians 13 for possible answers.)

- Based on your understanding of love, in what ways does our church's typical weekend service show (or not show) genuine love to the people who visit? In other words, would people who attend our church say they feel loved after they've spent their one weekly hour with us?

Optional Activity:

Use the continuum on page 51 of *Why Nobody Wants to Go to Church Anymore*, which is based on 1 Corinthians 13, to assess what the people who visit our church may experience.

- In what ways might two-way conversation make people feel loved at our church?

Look It Up *(15 minutes)*

Let's read this excerpt together from *Why Nobody Wants to Go to Church Anymore*:

> **"Radical as it sounds, churches need to allow time for participants to talk. We know that pastors and other leaders flinch at the thought, but sound education methodology understands that people of all ages can only absorb up to 10 minutes [most say only 6 minutes] of input at a time. It's true! So to be more effective—and practice Fearless Conversation—we must give others time to discuss, download, grapple, and debrief. All of this helps personalize the point and ensure it will stick."** (page 109)

Let's talk about this statement.

- Do you agree or disagree? What makes this truer today than ever?

- What part does conversation play in strengthening our relationships? Can you imagine healthy relationships without conversation?

- Why do you think it might be a good idea to allow people to share their personal stories, thoughts, and "wonderings" in church? And how could doing that on a regular basis change the dynamics of our ministry?

- Why do you think it's important to make our conversations "fearless"?

- Based on what we've discovered so far, in what ways is Fearless Conversation an act of love?

SESSION 3 | Fearless Conversation:
Are thoughts, doubts, and questions welcome?

37

- Do you have any friends or family members who've stepped away from church because their questions weren't welcomed? Tell about that.

Rise Up *(5 minutes)*

Action Plan Step 3

There's one simple thing we can do to transform our ministry. It won't cost a dime, and it will increase our relationship effectiveness exponentially. That one simple thing?

Let everyone talk.

During our next church service, Bible class, meeting, or team training, we need to allow some time (at least 5 minutes) to give everyone a chance to discuss or grapple with something said to the entire group. The leader can have people divide into groups of two or three, and then ask them a question that allows them to share their own thoughts and stories with their partners. And if we're feeling really brave, we can allow an extra few minutes for two or three people to report their responses to the entire group.

When We Did This

Sound scary? Be fearless! We've done this practice thousands of times in churches all over the world, and we guarantee that it not only works but works wonders.

Tell people why you're having them talk with a partner. If you've never been "fearless" like this before, we've learned people are very cooperative when they know why you're doing it. Let them know that we gain more when we're engaged, we learn and discover more when we talk things out, and that our interactive Internet world has trained us to participate. Everyone naturally knows how to converse.

Optional Challenge:

Give Fearless Conversations a try this week. Below is a list of questions you can use to spark a dialogue with someone you know. Invite someone to lunch or coffee and just be a friend. Next week, we'll take a few minutes as a group to debrief what happened.

- What's the greatest piece of wisdom ever passed on to you?

- What do you like most about what you do? Least?

- Why do you think there are so many different religions?

- What conclusions have you come to concerning life after death?

SESSION 3 | **Fearless Conversation:**
Are thoughts, doubts, and questions welcome?

- Have you ever been able to get a handle on what you think your purpose in life is?

- As you've watched or read the news, what conclusions have you drawn about the nature of humanity?

- Have you ever had an experience in which you felt the presence of God?

- What causes you to struggle the most with the idea of God's existence?

(Questions taken from *God Space* by Doug Pollock, published by Group. An additional conversation-starter resource is Group's digital app Gabbit.)

CONVERSATION TIPS

After some friendly chat and getting caught up with each other, you might preface one of these questions with something like, "You know, I've been wondering about some stuff lately and wanted to see what you think." Don't go into the conversation with an agenda; just talk. Listen. Hear what your friend has to say. Swap stories and experiences. Remember, you're not doing this activity to teach them or persuade them of anything. Simply practice the art of conversation.

Wrap Up *(5 minutes)*

Let's take a couple minutes to give our fears to God. Take turns praying one-sentence statements about things you might be afraid of or nervous about. If you have more than one, feel free to pray as many statements as you need.

[After everyone offers at least one statement, have one person in your group commit those fears to God and ask him to give you strength and courage as you conquer those anxieties. Pray that God will guide your Fearless Conversations this week.]

"God, we come to you because we love you and trust you, but we have fears…"

Next week we're going to explore the third Act of Love: Genuine Humility. Be prepared to share the results from your weekly challenge of having a Fearless Conversation. Be ready to explore how Genuine Humility can make our church irresistible.

41

SESSION 3 | Fearless Conversation:
Are thoughts, doubts, and questions welcome?

WHY NOBODY WANTS TO GO TO CHURCH ANYMORE
ACTION PLAN: Workbook for Your Ministry Team

SESSION 4

Genuine Humility:
Is everyone in our church in this together?

Reminder!

- Sections in regular font are meant to be read aloud by the facilitator to the entire group.

- Sections in **bold font** are intended to be read by the whole group.

- Sections within brackets [ ] are directions to the session facilitator and should not be read aloud.

Warm Up *(5 minutes)*

Welcome back! This is the fourth session of our in-depth Action Plan, and we're working toward finding practical ways to make our church a genuine haven for God's love. You're an important part in making this happen at our church—and for that, I thank you!

This week we're tackling the sometimes-touchy topic of Genuine Humility. Before we jump in, let's take a few moments to share something personal about ourselves. As a team, it's important that we're honest and vulnerable with each other. It's also essential that we care for each other and lift each other up.

SESSION 4 | **Genuine Humility:**
Is everyone in our church in this together?

43

Let's take turns answering the following question:

- What's one thing that keeps you humble?

Follow Up *(5 minutes)*

Let's share any interesting discoveries from last week's challenge. We were supposed to give people the chance to talk sometime during an event or worship time we led. Report any "ah-has" from your experience or from any conversations you had during the week.

Let's take 5 minutes to discuss these two questions:

- How do you think it went?

- Did people grow closer to each other as a result?

Open Up *(20 minutes)*

"Church people are a bunch of hypocrites" versus "We're all in this together."

Genuine Humility is all about putting God and others first. One of the best ways to keep your pride in check and gauge how well you love others with Genuine Humility is to weigh your priorities. For Christians and their church, love should be *the* top priority. (John 15:9-17, Mark 12:28-31, 1 Corinthians 13, and 1 John 4:19-21 make that very clear.)

Is love your priority? Does love win out when you make decisions about how to lead ministry? Is loving God *and* others the one thing around which every—*every*—part of our church revolves?

As a group, let's read through the following 10 pairs of statements and decide which one is a more honest reflection of our church. How would you truthfully answer each of these statements?

[Note: The choices here don't necessarily mean you must choose one and abandon the other. But when considering how you make every decision in ministry, something must always take priority. This list is meant to help you understand what your church's real priorities are.]

1. **What's more important:**

   That everyone in our church believe exactly the way we do?

   or

   That everyone in our church knows they will always be loved and supported?

2. **What's more important:**

   That people in our community know where our church stands on the issues?

   or

   That people in our community know our church will always welcome them?

3. **What are people more likely to hear from our church:**

We love God, and you should too.

or

We love God, and we love you too!

4. **What's more important:**

That people see our church's leadership team as mature, near-flawless believers?

or

That people see our church's leadership as real people who admit their mistakes and struggle with many of the same things they do?

5. **What's more important:**

That we enforce accurate doctrine and theology?

or

That we nurture healthy, Jesus-centered relationships?

6. **What's more important:**

That we protect our church from "serial sinners"?

or

That we acknowledge that everyone is struggling with something?

7. **What's more important:**

That our church is known for its professional, polished worship services?

or

That our church is known as a place of caring and kindness?

8. **What do people spend more time doing in our church:**

   Facing forward silently?

   or

   Facing each other and growing in relationships?

9. **What's more likely:**

   That our church takes care of its own interests?

   or

   That our church looks out for the personal needs of our community?

10. **What's more important:**

    That we're right?

    or

    That we love?

[After you've discussed your church's position for the above statements, read the quote below from Doug Pollock's book *God Space:*]

> **"Essentially, we are sending the culture this message: Not only do we not endorse your point of view, we also don't accept you. This lack of acceptance crushes opportunities for spiritual conversations. Acceptance does not mean endorsement. When we confuse the two, we destroy the very space God wants to work in."**

- How is acceptance different from endorsement? In what ways do we confuse the two?

SESSION 4 | Genuine Humility:
Is everyone in our church in this together?

47

- Why was "acceptance without endorsement" such a radical approach for Jesus?

- Why is it hard for Christians to show Jesus-style acceptance to the people of our culture?

When We Did This

We had people read John 3:16: "For God loved the world so much that he gave his one and only Son, so that everyone who believes in him will not perish but have eternal life." Then we asked them to read verse 17: "God sent his Son into the world not to judge the world, but to save the world through him." We then asked people: What light do these words shed on love? People love to share the "gospel in a nutshell" (the famous verse in 16)—but then forget to share the next verse—and condemn.

Wise Up *(10 minutes)*

Let's read a Scripture passage together and then talk about the following questions. This is Philippians 2:1-5:

"Is there any encouragement from belonging to Christ? Any comfort from his love? Any fellowship together in the Spirit? Are your hearts tender and compassionate? Then make me truly happy by agreeing wholeheartedly

with each other, loving one another, and working together with one mind and purpose. Don't be selfish; don't try to impress others. Be humble, thinking of others as better than yourselves. Don't look out only for your own interests, but take an interest in others, too. You must have the same attitude that Christ Jesus had."

- Most people read this passage on a personal level. Yet Paul wrote it to a group of people—a church. How is applying this Scripture different when applied to a church instead of a single person?

- How would you say our church is living up to the relationship standards in this Scripture passage? What are two or three key areas we could improve in?

- Focusing on relationships means *things* (church building, calendar, budget, etc.) will get messy. What specific actions can we do to stay committed to remaining genuinely humble (meaning, it's not about us)?

SESSION 4 | Genuine Humility:
Is everyone in our church in this together?

Look It Up *(15 minutes)*

Let's read aloud this excerpt together from *Why Nobody Wants to Go to Church Anymore:*

> **"What's so compelling about Genuine Humility?
> Genuine Humility requires us to 'do unto others as
> we would have them do unto us.' Would you want to
> be invited to someone's home only to have the host
> tell you that everything you think and do is wrong?
> We all have flaws and misdirected beliefs. We're all
> sinners. But most of us don't respond well when we're
> impugned rather than loved."** (page 141)

Why don't people feel like they belong in church? Thom and Joani's book lists several examples of what Genuine Humility is *not* in a church setting. Let's take turns reading each one aloud.

Genuine Humility is NOT:

- Bible classes and worship where people feel intimidated or humiliated. (Only pastors don't feel inferior in a room full of pontificators.)

- Puffed up, churchy language. (Don't assume everyone knows what you mean.)

- A place to hide. (Humility is transparency.)

- Property obsessed. (Declining churches worry more over replacing the carpet than changing lives.)

- A clique or club. (Many churches exude a country club mentality.)

- Sheep stealing and competitiveness. (Nobody cares about that but church teams.)

Now let's take a few minutes to discuss these questions.

- Of the list above, which has our church been most guilty of? Why do you think that is?

- How is admitting/confessing areas of weakness the beginning of Genuine Humility?

- How is treating people at church similar to the way you'd treat friends invited to your home? In the context of loving others, why should it be any different?

Rise Up *(5 minutes)*

Action Plan Step 4

Thankfully, practicing Genuine Humility is within everyone's grasp. A humble church, full of humble, loving people, would hardly ever be accused of being a bunch of judgmental hypocrites.

Here's our challenge for the week: Learn something from someone who is different from you. Find someone who doesn't go to church.

51

SESSION 4 | Genuine Humility:
Is everyone in our church in this together?

Or someone who's radically committed to a church that's way different than ours. Or someone who embraces a different political view or party. A neighbor you've never met. Or someone from another race or ethnic background. Maybe a transgender person. A homeless person. A witch.

Invite them to lunch or coffee…and do nothing but get to know them.

Be prepared to come back to the next session and share one or two things you learned from that person that helped you see the world in a different way.

Optional Challenge:

Conduct a "Rules Audit"

Walk through our church and look for signs. Are they people-friendly, or are the signs property-friendly? Do our signs protect our building, or do they promote relationships? Do our signs shout "No!" and "Off Limits!" or do they encourage unlimited interaction? This simple step is one of the easiest and most practical ways we can clean out everything that's not Genuine Humility from our church building.

When We Did This

This exercise surprised us! We found rule signs everywhere—the bathrooms, kitchen, hallways. When reading them through the eyes of love, uh, we had to laugh. Oops!

Wrap Up *(5 minutes)*

Let's say "yes" to Genuine Humility...together. We'll take turns reading aloud the following statements in an attitude of prayer. After each statement, answer by saying "yes" together (that is, if you're truly willing to commit to it).

- **Are we willing to be radically relational with the people in our church? (Yes!)**

- **Are we open to learning from others, even if their opinions and perspectives don't exactly align with ours? (Yes!)**

- **Are we willing to admit our mistakes and love others despite theirs? (Yes!)**

- **Are we willing to put people over buildings and rules? (Yes!)**

- **Are we willing to communicate openly and directly? (Yes!)**

Amen!

Next week we're going to explore the fourth Act of Love: Divine Anticipation. Be prepared to share the results from the weekly challenge. And be ready to explore how Divine Anticipation can make our church irresistible.

53

SESSION 4 | Genuine Humility:
Is everyone in our church in this together?

WHY NOBODY WANTS TO GO TO CHURCH ANYMORE
ACTION PLAN: Workbook for Your Ministry Team

Divine Anticipation:
Are you ready to connect with God in a fresh way?

Reminder!

- Sections in regular font are meant to be read aloud by the facilitator to the entire group.
- Sections in **bold font** are intended to be read by the whole group.
- Sections within brackets [ ] are directions to the session facilitator and should not be read aloud.

Warm Up *(5 minutes)*

Welcome! We're into the fifth session of our team's 4 Acts of Love Action Plan, and we've been exploring some radical new ways to transform our church into a place where people experience God's tangible love. We couldn't do this without you. You are awesome!

Today we'll be talking about Divine Anticipation and how it helps us love others in a very real way. Let's warm things up with an interesting question.

- Find a partner and share about a time when you saw God working in your life or in the world around you.

Would anyone want to share their story with the whole group?

[Allow time for responses.]

Did you notice how wonderful it felt to hear all those God stories? We were actually practicing Fearless Conversations. Yeah!

Follow Up *(5 minutes)*

Now let's share any interesting discoveries from last week's challenge. We were asked to learn something from someone who is different from us. We'll have 5 minutes to find a partner and take turns sharing our responses to this question:

- Who did you meet with; how are they different from you; and what did you learn?

Open Up *(15 minutes)*

"Your God is irrelevant to my life" versus "God is here ready to connect with you in a fresh way."

The experiences we just described are great examples of loving others with Genuine Humility. And an amazing thing happens when we humble ourselves—we allow God to do what God does best. That's where Divine Anticipation comes in.

Most of us talk about expecting God to work among us, but how often do we actually look for it? How often do we recognize God is active in our daily lives? How often do we trust God to be in control?

Let's pause for a moment. Take 2 minutes of silence to look around the room we're in right now [have one person keep time on a phone or watch]. Find at least one thing in this room you've never noticed before. It could be the pattern in the carpet, the colors outside the window, or a picture on the wall you've never really looked at. Anything.

[After the 2 minutes is up, discuss the following questions.]

- What did you see? Why do you think you've never noticed it before?

- How is this activity similar to the way we tend not to notice God's involvement in our everyday lives?

- In what ways may you have missed seeing God at work in our church recently?

When We Did This

Most of the stories we hear from people who experience Divine Anticipation have come from personal encounters and conversations they've had with others. Typically, people at church fixate on only what happened 2,000 years ago—or more. We talk about what happened "back then." People need to know God is real. Now. Divine Anticipation is usually played out in our everyday lives—through relationships, accomplishments, losses, joys, sorrows, and even casual encounters.

SESSION 5 | **Divine Anticipation:**
Are you ready to connect with God in a fresh way?

- In light of the fact that the majority of people say they don't experience God at church, what are some fresh ways we could incorporate Divine Anticipation in our church on a relational level?

Look It Up *(15 minutes)*

In *Why Nobody Wants to Go to Church Anymore*, Thom and Joani describe several ways we can recognize Divine Anticipation. I'll read the points on this list one at a time. After each point, we'll pause for a minute or two to answer these questions:

- In what ways has our church lived out this aspect of Divine Anticipation?

- In what ways could our church do this better?

Divine Anticipation is...

- realizing God is actively involved, all the time. (Like radio waves, we just need to tune in.)

- grasping our "God-power." (The same power that brought Jesus back from the dead is the same power working in and through us.)

- accepting there are things we just can't explain. (That's why we need faith.)

- trusting the Holy Spirit. (That means letting go of our own agendas and allowing God to do his work.)

- being relevant—realizing God is relevant to each person. ("Relevant" does not mean "cool.")

- expecting God to show up. (Where two or more are gathered in God's name, he's there with them.)

- trusting that God will do what only God can do. (The church tries so hard, but God is the one who makes things grow.)

- telling others—in an authentic, natural way—what God is doing in our own lives and the lives of others. (Remember, faith is a relationship.)

- allowing people to express their faith in their own way. (There's not one right way.)

SESSION 5 | **Divine Anticipation:**
Are you ready to connect with God in a fresh way?

Wise Up *(10 minutes)*

Let's read 1 Corinthians 3:5-7 together. Then we'll talk about the questions that follow.

> "After all, who is Apollos? Who is Paul? We are only God's servants through whom you believed the Good News. Each of us did the work the Lord gave us. I planted the seed in your hearts, and Apollos watered it, but it was God who made it grow. It's not important who does the planting, or who does the watering. What's important is that God makes the seed grow."

- Why do church leaders want to claim success from their hard work in ministry? How do you discern what's God's job and what's your job? What's the difference?

- How can we encourage ourselves and each other to allow God to make the growth happen?

WHY NOBODY WANTS TO GO TO CHURCH ANYMORE
ACTION PLAN: Workbook for Your Ministry Team

- How do we know growth when we see it? (We're *not* talking about growth in numbers.)

Rise Up *(5 minutes)*

Action Plan Step 5: God Sightings

Each day this week, look for a "God Sighting"—a way you've seen God at work in the world around you. Keep a piece of paper handy and write down each God Sighting you see every day. Next week our group will share the God Sightings we've written down.

Optional Challenges:

Plan a Surprise

Here's a chance to put Divine Anticipation to the test. At a church worship service in the near future, don't prepare a sermon or plan out your songs. Instead, spend your prep time in prayer. Turn the time over to asking people to share with a partner how they saw God working (or not) during the previous week. Then ask a few who are willing to share their stories with everyone. You will be surprised, challenged, and perhaps astounded at what happens. It will be a week few will soon forget.

When We Did This

Simply trusting God and listening to each other's stories is risky—yet incredible!

SESSION 5 | **Divine Anticipation:**
Are you ready to connect with God in a fresh way?

The Gorilla Test

To help your people understand how we need to look for God in our everyday life, show the "Gorilla" video from the enhanced digital version of *Why Nobody Wants to Go to Church Anymore*. The video asks the audience to count the number of times two jugglers are tossing a ball. Your people will be so focused on the jugglers that they won't see a man in a gorilla costume walk through the crowd. Make the point that God is present in our daily life—we just have to anticipate his involvement.

Wrap Up *(5 minutes)*

For the next 5 minutes, let's sit in prayerful silence. Listen to hear what God may have to say to you. It may be uncomfortable to sit quietly for that long, but let's give it a try as we bring this session to a close. Listening is an act of love, so let's love God right now.

[Listen in prayerful silence for 5 minutes.]

Amen.

Next week we're going to use our time to "look outward" and take the next big steps toward becoming an irresistible church. Be prepared to share the results from your weekly challenge of looking for God Sightings each day.

[Note: If possible, please conduct your next session in the main sanctuary of your church building.]

SESSION 6

Looking Outward:
What do we do now?

Reminder!

- Sections in regular font are meant to be read aloud by the facilitator to the entire group.

- Sections in **bold font** are intended to be read by the whole group.

- Sections within brackets [ ] are directions to the session facilitator and should not be read aloud.

[Note: If possible, please conduct this session in the main sanctuary of your church building.]

Warm Up *(5 minutes)*

Hallelujah! We've made it to the final session of our team's Action Plan for making our church irresistible. You are a blessing to this church! Thank you for being part of this exciting process. Let's take a few minutes to warm things up and take turns answering the following question:

- What's one thing you're really good at, and how did you become really good at it?

Follow Up *(10 minutes)*

It's time for God Sightings! Let's take some time now to share how you saw God working in the world around you this week. Then we'll take a few minutes to discuss two questions.

- How does it make you feel to hear stories from others about how they're noticing God's handiwork in their everyday lives?

- How do you think the rest of our church would respond if they had regular opportunities to hear how God is working in everyone's lives?

Open Up *(15 minutes)*

This study guide is called an "Action Plan" because it's all about *doing*. It's one thing to read a book and be inspired to make a change. It's something altogether different to make a change.

- So what does a church look like that embraces the concept of "faith as a relationship"?

Look It Up *(15 minutes)*

Let's read this excerpt together from *Why Nobody Wants to Go to Church Anymore:*

> "Be a matchmaker. What if we thought of our role as helping people fall in love with Jesus? Falling and staying in love with Jesus promises life, hope, passion, commitment, and joy—just like a great marriage. It's powerful. Merely doling out information about God isn't the source of that power. A real relationship with Jesus is. As matchmakers, it's *not* our job to *make* people Christians. Our role is simply to connect people to Jesus. We set up the date. God's grace lights the fire. And the Holy Spirit takes it from there." (page 206)

Let's talk about our role as a church leader, being a "matchmaker" for Jesus.

- How would you approach ministry differently if you embraced your role as someone whose sole purpose is to "connect people with Jesus"?

- Can you think of any roles on a church ministry team that should not be focused on strengthening people's relationship with Jesus? Explain.

- What would our church be like if our entire leadership team did nothing but act as "matchmakers" for Jesus?

- How does knowing that God is in control free us from trying to do more than connect people with Jesus?

Wise Up *(10 minutes)*

Let's dig into some Scripture together by reading 2 Corinthians 5:13-14, 20. Then we'll talk about the following questions.

> **"If it seems we are crazy, it is to bring glory to God. And if we are in our right minds, it is for your benefit. Either way, Christ's love controls us…So we are Christ's ambassadors; God is making his appeal through us."**

- If God is truly working through people, why do you think so many church leaders seem determined to accomplish and control things on their own?

- What do you think brings God more glory: Simply loving people? Or all the other things churches focus most of their time on (like buildings, higher attendance, and polished worship services)?

- If loving people brings God more glory, why do you think so many churches choose to focus on the other stuff?

- What does it mean to be "Christ's ambassadors"? How much do relationships have to do with it?

Rise Up *(5 minutes)*

Action Plan Step 6: Letting Go of the Numbers

Thom and Joani talk about how the "ABCs"—attendance, buildings, and cash—are the main distractions and misguided focus for most churches today. Let's explore how to get our church to distance itself from making the ABCs our primary focus. Just imagine: **What would our church be like if it left the ABCs behind and made the 4 ACTS OF LOVE the top priority?**

Look over the following ideas for getting us on the right path to placing attendance, buildings, and cash low on the priority list. As a group, let's choose as many of these ideas as we're willing to implement this week.

[Write them down, make copies for your team, and commit together to diminishing the stronghold of the ABCs.]

For each one we check off, we'll replace it with one new way we can emphasize growing relationships with each other and God.

☐ Quit measuring ourselves and our success by the numbers.

☐ Stop asking numbers questions, such as…

- "How many people come to our worship services or classes?"
- "Are we doing multi-site?"
- "How big is our youth group?"
- "How many staff do we have?"
- "What's our budget?"
- "How large is our campus?"

☐ Review our church newsletters and bulletins. How much space is devoted to financial reports and graphs or rules about building usage?

☐ Audit the sermons and pleas for money. How often do we find ourselves begging for dollars? Or worrying about repairing the roof? How often have we shared a life changed from one of our sermons?

☐ Check how much time and energy is spent in committee meetings haggling over new building campaigns, fundraising, paint colors, carpet choices, and paving the parking lot, compared to telling stories of lives touched because of our facility.

Optional Challenge:

Letting Go of Our Fears

The Bible says "fear not" 366 times. Fear is stifling the church in more ways than we can count. But we need not have any fear when we're focusing solely on growing people closer to Jesus.

Let's read through this list of fears together as a group. Take a pen or highlighter and mark the fears that you find yourself personally guilty of. Take a few minutes to pray silently to commit those fears to God, and then we'll take a few minutes to pray together as a group.

- Do you fear naysayers?

- Do you fear the new and different?

- Do you fear change?

- Do you fear doctrinal impurity?

- Do you fear factual purity?

- Do you fear deeper relationships with people and instead pursue relationships with ideas?

- Do you fear not knowing all the answers?

- Do you fear losing your job?

- Do you fear loss of control?

- Do you fear getting hurt?

- Do you fear being judged by colleagues or church members?

- Do you fear failure?

Wrap Up *(10 minutes)*

[Stand together as a group in the center of your church sanctuary. If you're not able to meet in your sanctuary, close your eyes and do your best to imagine you're there.]

One at a time, we'll look around the room and find something that represents what our church does on a regular basis. (For example, the microphone on the stage could represent our church's weekly sermons.) Then let's take 1 minute to share one-sentence ideas for how we can turn that activity into a way to grow relationships with Jesus and each other.

Someone can record the ideas on a flip chart; then we'll review the list of ideas and prioritize them into 5 to 10 activities that we will commit to work on in the weeks ahead.

[After finishing this activity, take a few minutes to pray together as a group, committing your team and yourselves to transforming your church into a place where love in action is always the priority.]

Thanks for being a part of this experience. The fact that you've committed to working on this Action Plan shows you care about our church. More importantly, it means that you're committed to loving God and others through your own life. I thank God for you!

WHY NOBODY WANTS TO GO TO CHURCH ANYMORE
ACTION PLAN: Workbook for Your Ministry Team

CONTINUE THE CONVERSATION

May God bless you on the next steps of your journey. Our team will be praying for you every day. Please let us know how you're doing! We love connecting with our friends in ministry and are eagerly waiting to hear the miraculous stories of faith and love in your church.

We give God thanks for you! For you are the church and together God's love will be real for others!

Hashtag: #WhyNobody

Facebook: facebook.com/WhyPeopleDontGoToChurch

Email: tschultz@group.com; jschultz@group.com

"Every time I think of you, I give thanks to my God. Whenever I pray, I make my requests for all of you with joy, for you have been my partners in spreading the Good News about Christ from the time you first heard it until now. And I am certain that God, who began the good work within you, will continue his work until it is finally finished on the day when Christ Jesus returns" (Philippians 1:3-6).

Thom & Joani Schultz

RESOURCES TO HELP YOUR JOURNEY

Why Nobody Wants to Go to Church Anymore
Video Enhanced eBook

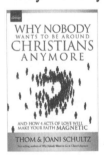

This video-enhanced eBook includes full color photography, links to additional content, and 28 videos. Discussion guides also available.

Why Nobody Wants to Be Around Christians Anymore

This book delivers practical advice and real-life examples of what it means to glow Jesus-style love that draws people to God instead of driving them away.

When God Left the Building

This documentary explores the state of the church in America—you won't be able to stop talking about it! If your church would like to host a showing, go to the website, click on "Cinema & DVD Alerts," and fill out the form. WhenGodLeftTheBuilding.com

God Space

A book to transform how you talk about your faith with others by Doug Pollock.

Fearless Conversation

An adult Sunday school curriculum designed to build relationships through authentic conversation.

Lifetree Café

A conversation café venue for an hour of stories and conversation to feed your soul. **lifetreecafe.com**

Holy Soup

Follow Thom Schultz's blog that challenges the church's status quo. **holysoup.com**